Pastors
Sound
Off

Pastors
Sound
Off

Causes We Can't Keep Quiet About

OPEN WATERS
PUBLISHING

© United Church of Christ, 2014

Open Waters Publishing
700 Prospect Avenue
Cleveland, Ohio 44115
openwaterspublishing.com

Design by Ted Dawson Studio

Printed in the United States of America

10 9 8 7 6 5 4 3 2 1

Open Waters Publishing is an imprint of The Pilgrim Press.
The Open Waters Publishing name and logo are trademarks
of Local Church Ministries, the United Church of Christ.

ISBN 978-0-8298-2022-5

CONTENTS

Introduction

People often write with unusual power and clarity when they write about what angers them, and that is certainly the case here. This booklet contains testimonies from pastors on causes they are passionate about. These are causes we just can't keep quiet about, so you might as well listen.

Everyone is particularly passionate about one social issue more than others. This means, of course, that not everyone is passionate about the same issue. It also means that not all important issues or causes are represented here.

We have different passions in much the same way we have different gifts—for the sake of the wider community. So I am grateful when someone is wild-eyed crazy about some issue, even if—or perhaps *especially* if—that is not the issue that stirs me up to the same degree.

One of the great things about testimonies is that you can lay them alongside each other and not try to reconcile them. You don't need to consider who is more right or persuasive than the others. Rather, read each entry in the way you would listen to a testimony. Receive each one as you would a gift.

One of the best ways to respond to a testimony is with a testimony of your own. Our hope is that, as you read these testimonies, you will discover—or rediscover—a cause that has your name on it. It might be one represented here or another cause entirely. Then we hope you will consider how your passionate convictions can be shared in ways that are a gift to others, as well.

Martin B. Copenhaver

The Unchallenged Voice of Christian Homophobia

Matt Fitzgerald

My church became Open and Affirming (ONA: extending full welcome of LGBT folks into the life and leadership of the church) more than twenty-five years ago. I was bragging about this to a friend. He replied, "Well, it's a liberal church right? Of course they thought it was okay to be gay."

I tried to stifle my annoyance. He seemed to share the widespread belief that the Christian right has the rules on its side: a Bible that says homosexuality violates God's will. Meanwhile liberal America has a political philosophy that holds the autonomous, self-sufficient person is able to do whatever he or she pleases. "Okay" is a liberal word. It refuses to pass judgment. "I'm okay and you're okay. It is okay to be gay. It is okay to be straight. You do your thing and I'll do mine and so long as no one gets hurt, what's the difference?"

This sounds good, but most Christians know that the kind of freedom liberals love will always reveal that we are flawed creatures who do selfish things, subjecting ourselves to what Stanley Hauerwas calls the "tyranny of our own desires."

Fortunately, God is still speaking. And while liberalism makes a good argument for the fact that homosexuality is *acceptable*, the Bible goes one step further to say quite clearly that gay people are *wonderful*. Not "okay" but "beloved." Not "tolerable" but "wonderfully made," as the psalmist puts it.

Open and Affirming churches ought to be clear that our status is neither a negative response to the Christian right nor a spiritual gloss for the left. Instead, it is a positive theological conviction. God creates some people gay, lesbian, bisexual. And because God declares creation good, gay people are therefore good.

Genesis doesn't say that God made straight people on the sixth day and gay people two weeks later. We are all children of the same creation. We are all children of the same creator. We are all in the church together. And refugees still come walking through our doors. Because even as many local congregations' ONA decisions retreat into the past, the loudest voices in Christendom refuse to get on board.

Twenty five percent of Americans are Roman Catholic. The official Catholic teaching on homosexuality labels LGBT sexual acts "intrinsically disordered." The catechism goes on to say, "They [homosexual acts] are contrary to the natural law . . . under no circumstances can they be approved." Pope Francis talks a good game, but his church is ruining peoples' lives.

The Southern Baptist Convention may be smaller than the Catholic Church, but they punch above their weight when it comes to hating LGBT people. "Homosexuality is not a 'valid alternative lifestyle.' The Bible condemns it as sin."

I know Jesus wants all Christians to be "one," but some of his people *enrage* me. As Christians we cannot sit idly by while the two largest Christian bodies in our country continue to condemn gay and lesbian people as a matter of both doctrine and practice.

I also know that as good liberal Protestants we are reluctant to make any absolute truth claims. "You believe what you want and I'll believe what I want and we'll all be okay." But the truth is that when it comes to the question of sexual orientation, the Catholics and the Baptists are wrong and we are right.

They are *hurting* people and we are *healing people.*
Now ask yourself, where do you think Christ is?

One of the reasons I know he is here is because I have seen my LGBT sisters and brothers carry him into church. Like anyone who has ever tried to follow Jesus, my faith wavers and grows weak. Left to myself I dither and doubt and question and get all wrapped up in the prospect of my own unbelief.

I was in the midst of such a time about nine months ago, and then a couple dropped into my office wondering whether they should join Saint Pauls. They had been chased out of their home church because they're gay.

They asked their home church, "Will you marry us?" They were told, "Of course not."

They asked their home church, "Will you baptize our children?" They were told, "Absolutely not, you shouldn't even have them."

They asked their home church, "Well, can we have communion on Sunday morning?

"They were told, "No. Not after you told us who you really are."

It seemed like a heartbreaking conversation. And it would have been heartbreaking if not for one thing. This family would not let go of Jesus. Or maybe God would not let go of them.

Either way, having witnessed this family's tenacious faithfulness, how can mine not grow in response? And having witnessed God's unrelenting commitment to God's LGBT children, how can my trust in God's faithfulness to all of us not grow?

We all have hurdles to clear in order to get to worship. Many of us have reasons to stay away from church, to write it all off as a disappointing institution that rests on a confusing myth. But not all of us have heard the church say "You are not welcome here." Not all of us need to challenge 2,000 years of liars who twist the truth to tell us we are "disordered." Not all of us have been told we are beyond the pale of salvation.

Only gay and lesbian Christians have to clear those hurdles in order to sing a hymn, teach Sunday School, feed the hungry, or share a cup of coffee in the church basement. In leaping into God's embrace over the obstacles our religion has placed in their path, our gay sisters and brothers teach the rest of us just what it means to be faithful. And so we learn to be faithful. And in our faith we're saved. By Christ, of course. But in my experience we ought to at least credit his LGBT sisters and brothers with the assist.

QUESTIONS FOR DISCUSSION

1. For centuries, Christian churches tended to ignore, misunderstand, or be hostile toward what we now refer to as LGBT issues of equality. The same could be said about the equality of women in religious life and society. What issues or concerns do you think we may be neglecting or ignoring now?

2. How is "coming out" similar to being "born again?"

3. What is the difference between "okay" and "beloved"? How and why does a Christian move beyond accepting another person to loving that person? Why is the liberal model of tolerance sometimes not enough?

4. Have you ever experienced obstacles to participating in church? Have you ever been told that you or a loved one is not welcome in church? What did you do?

5. When someone in the church makes a statement like "we are right, and they are wrong," what is your reaction?

Nobody Talks about Mental Illness

Anthony B. Robinson

Jesus told his disciples, "You did not choose me; I chose you."
Sometimes it is that way with issues of human need as well. They choose
us, or so it has seemed to me.

The issue of mental illness reached out and took hold of me when one
of my children—then a young adult—experienced a psychotic break
during a church mission trip in Central America. I am so grateful that I
had decided to accompany the youth group on that trip. Still, it was a
terrifying time, and a shattering one. When alone I wept uncontrollably for
the first and only time in my life. It was also a time when I experienced,
and utterly relied upon, God's daily grace and presence.

After that initial crisis the next two years were a time of passing
through some very deep water—for our son and for our family. Going with
us through the deep water were doctors, therapists and friends—and our
church. We chose to share with the congregation about the illness, in ways
that sought to respect our son and his privacy.

But this devastating experience and our disclosure of it opened some
amazing doors for learning and ministry. Our openness permitted and
encouraged that of others. As a pastor I began to discover how common

the experience of some form of major mental illness was for individuals and families in our congregation.

After the closet door had been broken open—mental illness may be the last illness so deeply shrouded with shame and secrecy—the congregation did several incredible things. Mental illness became a serious focus of adult education off and on over a several year period. Next, what we came to call "companions" were trained to do just that, to companion and walk alongside those struggling with mental illness. Our companions ministry meant we were better equipped to extend hospitality to those who came to us from the streets and shelters near our urban congregation, while also drawing boundaries for the health and safety of everyone in the community.

In time the congregation's response took an even more dramatic form. The relationships that had been built among those who had a family member with a mental illness, gave rise to a dream which became reality… a House of Healing. Members of the church found and renovated an old house turning it into a residential, spiritual community for eight people coming out of the public hospital's psych unit or ER, all of whom would, otherwise, have been thrust back on the streets of the city. The hospital staff screened referrals and provided case-management. We provided a home and a community. Today there are five of these "Houses of Healing," allowing residents up to two years in which to stabilize and re-establish connections.

At about the same time, I was given the opportunity to do other things because of this experience. I was asked to speak on mental illness in a variety of public settings, including legislative hearings. How did our systems of care and support work and how could they be improved? How might we as a society not only improve on our care and support to those who suffered mental illness, but also to their often overwhelmed and exhausted families? Next, I was invited by the National Alliance for the Mentally Ill to lead one of their new "Family to Family" groups. The group was for those who had a family member—a mother, son, brother, or spouse—who was experiencing mental illness. For me, that was a very rich experience, one that allowed me to use my own experience as a parent and also to use my gifts as a leader and facilitator.

What have I learned about mental health and illness as issues of justice and human need? That many of those who are homeless on our streets (perhaps 50% or more) suffer from a mental illness, often one that is untreated. Solutions aren't easy. But neither are such people beyond hope. In many cases, people can recover or learn to manage their illness. Turning a blind eye or cold shoulder is not an option for a moral community.

I've learned that many families who have a member who suffers from mental illness also live in a shadow land of disorientation and exhaustion. It is a place where few others visit. Often this isolation is magnified by secrecy and shame which families may inflict on themselves.

I've learned that the brain is an organ of the body and like other organs, it can become diseased or traumatized. Moreover, I've come to believe that most all of us have a potential to experience some form of mental illness under the right or wrong conditions.

I've also learned how important the ministry of the church is to people experiencing mental illness and to their families. Some churches may be called to provide services like the "House of Healing." Many churches can call and train companions who are on duty on Sunday mornings. The skills learned in that work are transferable to so many other areas of life.

But most of all I've learned how important community and relationship—relationship with God and other people—is to those who experience mental illness and to their families. For us, in the church, these are people, not patients. They are not reduced to a diagnosis or a label. They are "John," "Ben," or "Alice." They are baptized children of God.

And sometimes those who suffer mental illness teach us a harder, but necessary, lesson: not everyone or everything can be "fixed" or "cured." But even then our presence is still asked of us, and enabled for us, by a suffering God.

No, I didn't choose this issue or challenge. But this journey has helped me to grow as a disciple of Jesus Christ and for that I am deeply grateful.

QUESTIONS FOR DISCUSSION

1. How have perceptions about persons who experience mental illness changed in your lifetime—or have they?

2. Have you had personal experience of major mental illness (depression, bi-polar illness or schizophrenia) in your own life or that of a family member or close friend? What has that been like for you?

3. What kinds of mental health care and services exist for you and your family? What exists in your community for people whose health care coverage may be limited?

4. What role do you see for your church in relation to those who experience mental illness or their family members?

When it Comes to Income, We're Worlds Apart

Jason W. Coulter

Before I became a minister, I worked for thirteen years as a union organizer.

I worked with the people who laundered tablecloths and napkins for restaurants in Cleveland, with distribution-center workers who packed mail order boxes in Indianapolis, and with textile workers in North Carolina who manufactured sheets and towels. At each stop along the way, I was invited into the workers' lives. By sitting on couches in living rooms and pulling up chairs around kitchen tables, I got an unvarnished glimpse of American pain. And an unvarnished view of human hope.

I remember the lady in Greenfield, Ohio, who collected penguins, and had just about every possible permutation of penguin crammed into the living room of her house trailer. Outside of Iron Mountain, Michigan, I had a cup of coffee with a foundry worker and a mouse. The mouse quietly nibbled at a piece of toast on the table as the man and I talked about the raises he and his co-workers never saw.

In Chicago, I paid a visit to the Robert Taylor Homes housing project to sign up a worker from one of the city's industrial laundries. Her family had painted the cinder-block walls of their apartment every single color under the sun. It was like a Sherman Williams truck had exploded in their living room. The kaleidoscope colors were bright and joyous—in sharp contrast to the dull yellow urine-stained corridors that led to the door of their apartment.

These days, my work as a pastor can take me to altogether different places. Last summer I attended a reception in one of Chicago's toniest suburbs, at the home of a major donor to a not-for-profit that does important work in our community. He is a vice-president of a major corporation. And his wife is an investment banker. And their home is a palace. They may not be in the 1% but they sure can see it from their front porch.

After dinner, they gave us a tour of their place. As one room spilled into another we traveled through their home until we arrived at what she called her "mask room"—an entire room dedicated to her collection of tribal masks and artifacts that they had collected in their world travels. The colors in the masks were just as varied as those on the wall of that apartment in the projects. Only the urine yellow was missing. When we wrapped up the tour, I thought to myself, "How do laundry workers and investment bankers share the same planet, much less the same nation?"

Income inequality and the vast disparities in wealth are one of the most pressing challenges confronting our democracy. The last thirty years have seen an increasing concentration of wealth in the hands of a very few, while vast swaths of our population have seen their wages stagnate. According to the Economic Policy Institute, the average net worth of the 400 richest Americans—the much-discussed "1%"—increased from $1.1 billion to $3.8 billion from 1982 to 2011. Their collective wealth now totals *$1.7 trillion*, which exceeds the wealth of the 80 million Americans at the bottom end of the scale. Wages for CEOs have increased by 725% over a similar time period, while pay for private sector workers rose a measly 5.7%. Not only are the rich getting richer, the poor are getting poorer. There isn't a gap between the two Americas—there is a chasm.

How can this be? There is no single cause, but many; the rise of the information economy and the decline of manufacturing, tax policies that favor those with high incomes, the declining power of unions, and the disparities that exist in our education system are among those most often cited. As a nation we claim that all persons are created equal, but it is clear that all are not afforded equal opportunity. The resulting inequality is wrong and threatens the well-being of our country.

What can we do? To whom can we look for guidance? I suggest we steer clear of economists and policy wonks and instead incline our ears to the prophets of old. The Hebrew prophets Amos, Isaiah, and Micah confronted societies hundreds of years before the birth of Christ that had similar disparities in wealth. They did not issue white papers or offer press releases. They proffered powerful condemnations of those who enriched themselves at the expense of the poor. Feel the holy rage in the words of Amos:

> Hear this, you that trample on the needy, and bring to ruin the poor of the land, saying, "When will the new moon be over so that we may sell grain; and the sabbath, so that we may offer wheat for sale? We will make the ephah small and the shekel great, and practice deceit with false balances, buying the poor for silver and the needy for a pair of sandals, and selling the sweepings of the wheat." The Lord has sworn by the pride of Jacob: Surely I will never forget any of their deeds. Shall not the land tremble on this account, and everyone mourn who lives in it . . . ? (Amos 8:4-8a)

Amos and the prophets offered a vision of a world in which the abundance of God would not rot in the storehouses of the rich, but be shared with the widow, the orphan, the immigrant. A world in which a laundry worker, or a hotel housekeeper, or a nurse's aide might more fully share in the blessings that God has showered on this nation.

The investment banker who hosted us in her home wasn't a bad person. She is generous and gives her time and money to not-for-profits that make the world a better place. She was a hard-working American, just like the stone-broke foundry worker. But she was soaring on rotten wings.

What if I had told her about the piss-stained hallways that are found just miles from her mask room? What if I told her that just one of her rare masks could feed a thousand families in the projects? What if I had raged like a prophet, condemning the fruit rotting in her storehouse? I didn't do it. Like most church people I value niceness more than truthfulness. But Amos didn't. And perhaps we can't afford to any longer.

QUESTIONS FOR DISCUSSION

1. A capitalist society will always have differences in economic outcomes among individuals in society. How much difference, or inequality, is tolerable? When does it become intolerable?

2. Who has the greater responsibility for addressing inequality—government or individuals? Are there limits to what governments or individuals can accomplish?

3. What role does anger, or righteous frustration, play in motivating you to do justice? How can anger be helpful? How can it be hurtful?

People Who Can't
Love Jesus Without
Dissing the Jews

Mary Luti

I'd just sat down to write this essay when, procrastinating on Facebook, I noticed yet another blog post by yet another Christian writer slandering the Jews. And I'm not talking about fundamentalist writers. I'm talking about my own kind— "progressives." This one affirmed that Jesus came to lift the Law's yoke from a people hopelessly burdened by its legalistic minutiae. Others assert similar things—Jesus routinely violated Judaism's taboos against associating with women. He broke the silly Sabbath rules. His defiance of the "religious system of his day" got him killed.

The problem with these assertions is that they're based on a faulty picture of Judaism. The joyless, oppressive religion Jesus supposedly flouted is largely a straw man, set up in the polemics between Jews and Christians as they went their separate ways in the generations after the destruction of the Temple in 70 C. E. Those propagandists flung tons of mud at each other in that painful process of differentiation. Some Christian mud stuck to the emerging gospels. Their negative picture of Judaism hardened into stereotypes that have fueled the engine of Christian contempt ever since—Jews as legalistic, futilely striving to earn God's approval, blind to the obvious, oppressive of women, the disabled, and "sinners."

Christians are also largely ignorant of the ways Jews regarded the Law. We assume that if Leviticus says, "Thou shalt kill rebellious children," that's what people did. We know little of oral traditions that contextualized the Law in practice, differences of opinion among Jewish interpreters, and developments in Jewish thinking that stemmed from disputing together. Such ignorance is the wellspring of a sometimes unconscious but always harmful anti-Judaism in our preaching and teaching. Who doesn't dislike a religion that kills rebellious children? Never mind that it may not be true.

When I hear Christians repeat this stuff, it makes me sad. But I'm not innocent. When I was growing up, I thought Jesus set himself against his own religion too; so much so that it was easy for me to believe he was not a Jew at all. And because I knew exactly one Jew back then, a boy in my class, I also thought modern Judaism was like the unappealing "pharisaical" religion of the gospels. I felt sorry for that boy. And superior. "Thank you, God," I might have prayed, "that I'm not like the kid in the kippah."

But something wonderful happened to me in middle age. I got involved in interfaith conversation. I got to know "real" Jews. I went to services, Sabbath dinners, Seders. I learned that Judaism has always been wonderfully diverse. Then one night I found myself at a Simchat Torah service, a night of dancing with the scrolls to celebrate the completion of the annual cycle of readings, a festival of thanksgiving for the Law— the Law I thought Jews obeyed obsessively and which they found so burdensome they longed to be liberated from it by something like the grace of Jesus, who (perversely) they'd "rejected."

But nobody in that room appeared obsessed or burdened. They rocked the scrolls to and fro, passed them from hand to eager hand, and kissed them to delighted shouts and delirious song. Not a gloomy face anywhere, just the glistening sweat of dancing. That was when I resolved to learn as much as possible about the ways Christians misread Judaism and the Jews.

Now, if you think I'm making this up—that many progressives seem indifferent to the problem of Christian anti-Judaism—I give you the reaction to a daily devotional I wrote called "Bearing False Witness." I got more pushback on that piece than any other I've ever written. Some people got it, but most were either uncomprehending—I have no idea what you're talking about—or defiant. One sad flatly, "No. You are wrong." Another said his faith was staked on a Jesus who opposed the "dehumanizing and oppressive religion" of his day. He accused me of whitewashing Judaism. Another person was amazed that I suggested we learn from Jewish scholars of the New Testament. She saw no reason to let Jews tell her how to read her scriptures.

That piece hit a nerve. Clearly, progressive Christians need Jesus to embody our concerns. We look for a progressive Jesus in the gospels, and we find him—open, inclusive, impatient with schemes that dehumanize God's children, laser-focused on justice and love, not doctrine and rules. But this selective reading risks caricaturing Jews as benighted, Judaism as oppressive, and Jesus as a Christian hero. Our progressive Jesus comes at a price.

I wish we were unwilling to pay it. I wish we just let some things about Jesus be intractably odd, even unpalatable. I wish we accepted a fully human savior who spoke, ate, prayed, dressed, sang, loved, danced, taught, and died not as a liberation theologian or a progressive Christian, but as a first-century Jew.

We'll always find God's choice to enter human history in this limited, localized way discomforting. We have little choice but to live with it. But I wish we'd do more than live with it. I wish we'd gratefully embrace it. It's a key to our salvation.

The more I learn about Jesus' religion, the more I'm convinced I can love him without dissing the Jews. The more I see him through Jewish eyes, the more I'm convinced I don't have to bear false witness against my Jewish neighbors to bear true witness to his power in my life. The more I let him be the Jew he was, the better Christian I become.

These are good reasons to take anti-Judaism seriously. But even without them, I'd still insist we do. Our bloody history of calumny against the Jews—which includes the Holocaust—makes it unthinkable for us to remain unaware, defensive, or indifferent. Letting this slide has consequences.

We learned this nasty stuff; we can unlearn it. It'll take time—the habit of contempt is so ingrained. But it's never too late to begin.

QUESTIONS FOR DISCUSSION

1. When was the first time you had a clear understanding that Jesus was a Jew? Has that understanding made any difference in the way you think about his teaching and ministry?

2. Do you regard Jesus as a "counter-cultural" figure, at odds with the religion of his time and place? If so, where do you find him acting this way in the scriptures? Does the way you interpret such stories make Jews or Judaism look silly or narrow-minded or inhumane? Do you believe they were, or are?

3. Have you ever read the gospels with a well-informed Jewish friend? What difference might it make to do so?

Fracking the Poor

Quinn G. Caldwell

My father was a pacifist farmer; my mother, something of a mystic. They both loved the land: my father for what he and it could produce together, my mother for the way it made her feel. Dad believed in taking care of the earth because he knew in a deeply personal way how much we needed it: it produced the crops that fed the cows that made the milk that paid the bills. Mom believes in it because she experiences land as beautiful and mysterious. I remember my father ranting about some random guy's poorly-managed pasture as we drove by. I remember my mother crying for a week when they cut down the big old sugar maple in front of our house.

I grew up ranging through the fields and forests near my home. Some of the best memories of my childhood center on the times I spent hanging out in the woods with my Boy Scout troop. Some of the best memories of my adolescence involved sneaking around with friends, trespassing to go swimming in the clear waters at the feet of impossibly beautiful waterfalls.

I lived in the highlands of Bolivia for a time as a young adult, a fragile landscape that, unlike the place I grew up, had been deeply wounded by a long series of short-sighted environmental mismanagement. Deforestation, overgrazing, poor planting techniques, and more have ravaged the mountainsides until they literally slide away when it rains. There I learned that every environmental disaster is also a human disaster: it was not the middle or upper classes that bore the brunt of this degradation; it was the peasants, who were my friends and adopted family.

I tell you all of this not because I imagine it makes for particularly interesting reading, but because I tend not to trust people who get involved in social struggles on a purely theoretical—even a theological—basis. It's not that I doubt people can do good simply because they believe it's the right thing to do. It's that I've found that the people with real staying power in a struggle are the ones with a personal stake in it, people who believe that their parents or friends or selves have been or will be materially affected by the outcome. Don't tell me what you think the right thing to do is; tell me what you or your loved ones will lose if it goes wrong.

These days, I and my family spend a lot of time worrying about—some of us struggling against the advent of—fracking. "Fracking" is short for "hydrofracturing," a process that involves injecting water and chemicals into the ground under unbelievably high pressure to extract cheap natural gas, heretofore inaccessible in my part of the world, but now potentially highly abundant. The problem is that, while most of the water and chemicals and natural gas come out of a fracking well right where they're supposed to, no one really knows where else they might end up: ground water, ponds on small family farms, the clear waters at the feet of impossibly beautiful waterfalls. Stories abound of massive die-offs of flora and fauna in watercourses in areas where fracking is common. Some people, they say, can quite literally light their well water on fire as it comes out of their kitchen taps. The gas companies promise jobs and prosperity for those who live in areas where they will work; perhaps they're right. On the other hand, if it goes wrong, it will be the peasants that suffer. And that means my family, my Boy Scout troop, and me.

To my mind, the struggle to protect the environment God gave us, whether it be local as in the case of the fracking debate or global as in the case of the warming of the planet, is the most important struggle of our time. If the planet becomes less habitable, the pressures of those changes will be borne, as always, by the poorest, the weakest, and the least powerful. All the other issues over which we struggle—violence, economic inequality, gender, and the rest—will just get worse. And if it gets bad enough, if the planet becomes totally uninhabitable, then none of our other struggles will matter in the least.

QUESTIONS FOR DISCUSSION

1. What's one cause or issue you care about in a personal way, because of its effects on you or someone you love? What's one you care about in a theoretical way, because you think you should? How are they different? Which one matters more to you?

2. Quinn claims that questions of environmental sustainability are more important than any other, because without a livable planet, no other issue will matter. Do you agree? Why or why not?

3. Do you think God cares about the environment? Why or why not?

Sloppy Thinking about Immigration

Donna Schaper

They pick our lettuce and wash our strawberries. They care for our elders and our children. They start businesses and wash dishes in restaurants. They ride without helmets to deliver pizzas, especially in the rain when people don't feel like going out. They are not a "they;" they are a "we."

Unfortunately immigrants and the subject of immigration have turned into something about "them," as though my family hadn't immigrated to America or taken land from the natives. When we melt into a "we," the "problem" of immigration will turn into the opportunity of immigration. We will morph out of fear into something like fun, where immigrants, even our fearful selves, will be understood as a blessing, not a burden.

I don't pretend to understand policy or legislation or "pathways" to citizenship. I have worked for the comprehensive immigration bill for at least ten years now, my Senator knows me by name, as do all the electeds and the head of ICE (Immigration Control and Enforcement, an ugly name itself) in the greater NYC area. They know me by name because I know some immigrants by name. We are engaged in the legislative process but transformed by our experience in the New Sanctuary Movement.

We have met Jean, originally from Haiti and now an American. He was on the edge of deportation and pulled back by a movement that loved him too much to let him go. A national hero, he now works a van business and leads others to knowing they are a blessing and not a burden, while being a superb father to four American-born children, among whom are two honor students. We also met Fatamatou, whose husband was deported and who now cares for her six children in a community of women who have been the victims of genital mutilation and don't want to return to Kenya, even if it means their husbands will never see their children or their wives. We met Joe, who almost got deported only to get a reprieve (his wife and mother of his three children does not have one yet). He built a Chinese restaurant in Brooklyn that supports 32 workers. We met Ravi, who had been in prison for white-collar crime and while there became the unordained chaplain. The latest version of the comprehensive immigration reform bill would not change the possibility that Ravi would be deported. He did a crime, he did his time, and now he may still be deported, American wife and home and life notwithstanding. Why the double jeopardy? Why be punished twice for one crime? Because of the fictional "them" that needs to melt into a "we." Following that melt, the law will be changed. Before it, it won't.

Why don't we think our way to a sense of "we" in this great nation of immigrants? Because we listen to immature understandings of the "law" and refuse the mature understandings of broken laws. We not only have a broken legal system. It appears not to know how to forgive itself for its mistakes. Mature people love and forgive. Immature people forgive and go limp in the face of moral and legal complexity.

Immigration "laws" developed in a hodgepodge way. They are unenforceable; they involve "border controls" to borders that cannot be controlled. No one knows what the laws really are. They are episodically enforced. The laws are mistaken. They need to change so that citizens can have respect for laws—a valid moral position—and not become cynical about how dumb and unenforceable they are. I understand respect for the law but not respect for mistaken laws.

In addition to the legitimate if immature quandary about the law, multiple mythologies abound about immigrants. They are myths, not realities.

Consider these myths:

Immigrants do economic harm to citizens. They take our jobs.
Immigrants have anchor babies and are overpopulating America.
Immigrants have a higher crime rate than American nationals.

Each of these statements is factually false. There is a sneaky racism and an even sneakier spiritual imperialism involved in letting people say things that aren't true. I call it the Host/Guest conundrum. It goes back to the "we" and "they" issue. When people say that "they" take our jobs, someone needs to ask whose jobs are they in the first place? Does Ohio somehow own jobs and Mexico not? Why does capital get to move with impunity from South Carolina garment workers to Chinese garment workers and people can't? Who is the Host and who is the Guest on the great and single globe?

Scripture actually favors the guest. Leviticus 19:33-34 tells us that "When an alien resides with you in your land, you shall not oppress the alien. The alien who resides with you shall be to you as the citizen among you; you shall love the alien as yourself, for you were aliens in the land of Egypt: I am the Lord your God." Jesus continues this when he says in Matthew 25: 31-46: "when was it that you saw a stranger and welcomed him . . . . Truly I tell you, just as you did it to one of the least of these who are members of my family, you did it to me." Jesus is telling us where to find him and where to find God. One place is in the stranger.

Simultaneously, God is found in the stranger. "Often we entertain angels unaware." These strong "shoulds" telling us that we can find God and Jesus in the stranger continue throughout the gospels.

Our scriptures find their grand summation in the golden rule, meant to supplant all the rules and even the law. Our hope is that the golden rule *becomes* the law as opposed to hassling it. That rule is that "You are to love God above all and your neighbor as yourself." You don't get to stop loving your neighbor at the border of your country. You are to love your neighbor. Otherwise we miss God passing by.

It is easier, at first glance, to live as a host on the globe. Indeed, we are all guests.

QUESTIONS FOR DISCUSSION

1. Where are you ethically torn about immigration? Head straight to your own conflict. Try to name it and find one person to discuss it with this week.

2. Why do you think the country is divided on the subject of immigration? What are the stakes?

3. What could you or your church do to help an immigrant or an immigrant family? How could you be welcoming?

Enlisting Jesus as Either a Republican or a Democrat

Matt Laney

My Christian faith has two roots.

The first root comes from my father, a deep thinker who had an abiding love of the Bible. Dad went to seminary in the late 1960's at the height of the "God is dead" movement, which, as best I can tell, never got past Good Friday. We were frequent fixtures in the pews of a mainline Protestant church where we paid homage to our founder and gleaned "thoughts for the day" aimed at helping us live better lives.

The second root comes from a strong evangelical youth group where outstanding Christ-centered leadership, supplemented with heavy doses of preaching by Tony Campolo, caused me to fall head-over-heels in love with Jesus. But my nascent relationship with Jesus tacked left when many evangelicals were outed as homophobic and narrow-minded in a host of other ways.

In other words I'm something of an anomaly.

I love the mainline church but I often wonder if we are still Christian. I love evangelical piety even though it sometimes comes across as saccharine and insular. Liberal Christians find me too evangelical while evangelical Christians find me too liberal. My history in the church is one of feeling almost constantly out of place. However, such a vantage point has its advantages. For one thing, the saviors of each camp appear to be little more than divinized reflections of our polarized culture.

You know the contours of the following caricatures very well, but let me sketch them for you one more time:

Liberal Christians believe Jesus was kidnapped by the religious right during the Reagan administration. Blindfolded, bound and bedraggled, Jesus is now imprisoned in a dingy church basement somewhere down south because he refused to cosign their anti-gay, pistol-packing, welfare-slashing, free-market-capitalism-loving, selectively pro-life, agenda. In his place they propped up a triumphant, muscular, savior sporting a red, white and blue robe.

Meanwhile conservative Christians feel Jesus was hijacked by left-leaning strategists of the Democratic Party from Cambridge or Seattle who fancied him a modern day hippie-humanist-communist, occupy-ready peace-freak. The recent bumper sticker says it all: "Obama is not a foreign, brown-skinned anti-war socialist who gives away free healthcare. You're thinking of Jesus!"

Will the real Jesus please stand up?

Was Jesus a liberal or a conservative? A Green Party icon or a Tea-Party wannabe? Was Jesus apolitical? The answer isn't clear. Jesus is a spiritual Houdini when it comes to locking him into one of our modern cages.

What I know for sure about Jesus is this: he was passionate about undermining oppressive power structures beginning with the grip of sin on every human life. He was after total revolution, one heart at a time. He was a liberator but not a liberal. He was for tradition but not a conservative.

Here are some other things Jesus was (and is) not:

Jesus was not simply a great person. There have been many incredible people in the course of history, even in very recent times: Gandhi, Martin Luther King, Mother Teresa, Desmond Tutu. Their lives have inspired millions, but you don't hear anyone calling them the bread of heaven or the king of kings. Next to Jesus, they all considered themselves way down the ladder. If by some miracle I found myself standing in front of Martin Luther King, Jr. today, I would be in awe. But when Jesus enters the room, I would get down on my knees. Martin too. That's the difference.

Jesus was not only a great teacher. He told marvelous stories that put some in their place and lifted others to places they thought they didn't belong. But Christianity is not about offering a new teaching as if all we needed were better instructions.

Jesus is not fire insurance. When Jesus said he is "the way, the truth and the life" that *does* mean Christianity is about heaven but it's not about "going to heaven when you die." Christian faith comes with eternal benefits, but reducing Jesus to a ticket into heaven or to personal prosperity entirely misses the point.

In short, Jesus is not about morality, knowledge, or going to heaven. Those are the perks, but they're not the heart of the matter.

So what is?

The heart of the Christian faith is looking to Jesus as our savior. It's about being lost but now I'm found, blind but now I see, dying and being reborn, drowning and being tossed a line. It's about the fact that I've fallen and I can't get up.

Progressives often struggle with that. We're all for healing the world but less inclined to admit we also need a healer. We see the sickness and widespread dysfunction in our culture, but we tend to see ourselves as the enlightened exceptions.

We readily affirm that dentists cannot put fillings in their own teeth, a hairstylist cannot adequately do his own hair, a surgeon cannot operate on herself. We know we cannot baptize ourselves or serve ourselves communion. But we still struggle to admit that our lives are unmanageable, and that we can only be restored to sanity by belonging to a personal presence larger and wiser than ourselves.

Part of me would rather believe I can improve myself through my own efforts: a spiritual tweak here, a moral upgrade there, instead of admitting I need a total overhaul of heart and mind. Here's why: If I am healed by my own efforts, there would be limits to what God could ask of me. But if I am healed by the grace of God in Christ, then I belong to Christ and I owe God everything.

Ulp.

That's scary until we realize there is nothing more liberating than giving everything to God and nothing more terrifying than being left to our own devices. Giving up control is frightening until we admit we've never been in control for a day in our lives. That is the glorious surprise that comes with being liberated by a Christ who will never be bound by us.

QUESTIONS FOR DISCUSSION

1. When have you observed Jesus being used as spokesperson for either side of our politically divided culture? What does that say about our culture? What does that say about Jesus?

2. Has Jesus come into your life? If so, how were you introduced? If not, what have you learned about Jesus in Matt's essay that you would like to investigate further?

3. Who is Jesus, and why is he important?

Contempt for Religion has Become an Acceptable Prejudice

Lillian Daniel

I'm tired of listening to people trash religion in ways they would never trash anything else. I'm particularly annoyed when it is done by people who consider themselves open minded and prejudice-free.

I used to be kinder when people bashed religion. After all, the things they criticized were usually the same things I would criticize. It's a long list: abuse, sexism, fundamentalism, self-righteousness, superiority, hypocrisy and bad coffee. What kind of idiot would I be to defend any of that? So I just went along, nodding apologetically, perhaps piling on with more. "Hey, don't forget the Crusades, suicide bombers and the witch burnings. Hate those too."

I thought that if I listened to them bash religion and its excesses, they might realize that not all religion was like that. They might see that you can be in a tradition and still be critical of it. They might see that the tradition is more complicated and nuanced than they think. I could explain, "Look, we hate the same things you do. See? Now do you still hate us?"

But when you listen to people make blanket statements about something you care about and then agree with them, they tend to think that . . . well . . . you agree with them.

So I decided to move to the next phase of active listening, and pull out the secret weapon that would melt the heart of the random religion basher: the heartfelt apology. Oozing empathy, understanding and embarrassment, I would take it upon myself to apologize on behalf of every stereotype the religion basher held, thus revealing a self-perspective that would undermine their stereotype in the first place. Brilliant, right? Watch the magic happen: "Yeah, I hear you. The Crusades. Awkward. Not a good call. Sorry about that. We're against that now, by the way. But I hear you, I really do."

It turns out that the heartfelt apology on behalf of people you yourself find abhorrent doesn't really work. Apparently, when you apologize for the ordination policies, practices and histories of all the worst moments in religious history, your listeners feel their stereotypes affirmed, not challenged. Apparently, bathing religion bashers in niceness doesn't wake them up to the fact that they are spouting prejudice.

I'm tired of apologizing for a church I'm not a member of. And I'm tired of listening to people paint all religions with a bigoted brush.

These days, I am pushing back. When people make these blanket statements about the church, based upon one group of examples, and then paint the whole with that one part, I tell them there's a word for that. It's stereotyping.

The Crusades? Really? The Spanish Inquisition? You want me to apologize for that and nod politely when you take those examples and use them to smear my little community hundreds of years later? No thank you.

Instead I will point out that every human institution is flawed, mostly based on the fact that we allow human beings to join them. I might also point out that saying you won't go to church because it is full of hypocrites is like saying you won't go to the gym because there are out of shape people there. And lastly, I might repeat back to them some of the offensive things they have said, but use something else as a target, just so that they can hear it in a new way. Let's say that instead of speaking about religion, I used their words to talk about education. The argument might go something like this:

"I went to high school, and I was miserable in high school."

"Oh, I'm sorry. Why were you miserable?"

"I had a mean teacher. The other kids were mean, not interested in learning, just going through the motions.

"And I had a teacher who diminished me and didn't celebrate my gifts.

"Here's what really kills me: those teachers who say, 'I want to teach you chemistry.' They don't care if you learn about chemistry! They're getting rich by teaching chemistry and convincing me, 'Oh, you need to learn chemistry from me because I'm so special, because I studied it.' That's offensive. I understand chemistry. I experience chemistry in nature. It's like chemicals and flowers and the wind.

"Actually, when you look at all of the world's leaders and all of the politicians who have taken us into various wars, they all had some kind of education. When you look at it that way, education is the cause of all of the wars in the world. I really think education needs to be abolished."

If someone said that to you, you would think they were nuts. And if they stuck with it, you'd find them offensive. It's just a crazy way of talking that we would not tolerate in any other context. And yet we often do tolerate it when it comes to religion, especially in the liberal church, where we appropriately want to be open-minded and tolerant. We want to welcome people, and welcome their ideas. But would you welcome that kind of stereotyping about another group of people?

Look, I can't speak up for all of Christianity any more than I can speak for all of high school. But I can take notice when sloppy thinking slides into stereotyping.

Don't tell me what Christianity is like. I am a Christian and the church I belong to isn't like that. Don't tell me that all religions are the same. You don't know that. Don't tell me that questions of faith are responsible for all the wars in the world. That's ridiculous. Don't tell me that people of faith are mindless lemmings. That's insulting. I will call you on it.

I am tired of apologizing for a church I am not a member of. I will not allow contempt for religion to be the one acceptable prejudice. This prejudice, like all others, demands a frank and courageous response.

QUESTIONS FOR DISCUSSION

1. Have you ever heard someone bash religion in broad strokes and stereotypes? Can you give an example, not just from a public figure but from a personal conversation or interaction? Did you respond? If not, why not? If you did respond, what did you say? Do you wish now that you had said something different?

2. Does it feel different to listen to someone who has been personally hurt by a religious community? How does your response change?

3. Is there a way to acknowledge the flaws in religious communities but at the same time explain why your particular religious community matters to you?

Pretending We're Post-Racial

Kenneth L. Samuel

"To be black and conscious in America is to be in a constant state of rage."
–James Baldwin

Though it is not often spoken outwardly, virtually every black person in America who knows the struggles of black history and the racial challenges of black existence can attest to James Baldwin's blunt assertion. What most black people were taught, at an early age, is that black rage, though justified, will not allow acceptance into the institutions and socio-political settings that determine the socio-economic existence of black life in America.

The last person white America wants to deal with is an angry black person, while at the same time, most white Americans are unwilling to face the causes of black anger. Thus, a great part of being successful as a black American is the ability to suppress and deny black rage to the extent that white Americans are made to feel comfortable.

Having been raised in the slums of New York City, I was blessed to have a mother who cared about me enough to discipline me. And I was blessed to have a 7th through 9th grade English/Homeroom teacher who was committed to my personal as well as my academic development. Under their discipline and direction, I was awarded an "A Better Chance" scholarship that took me out of the ghettoes of the South Bronx and allowed me to matriculate at a premiere private college preparatory Catholic school, situated on 300 acres of rolling hills and lakes in northern New Jersey.

Out of high school, I was awarded full scholarships to Cornell University, the University of Pennsylvania and Wesleyan University. I chose to matriculate at Wesleyan. Majoring in African American History, my undergraduate education gave me an understanding of the history and policies that contributed to the existence of institutional racism and the creation of racial ghettoes, like the one in which I grew up. But when I attempted bring my knowledge of racism and my anger about racism into a student-led campaign designed to agitate against a specific racial injustice, I was cautioned against doing so by university personnel, who told me that I had too much to lose.

The year of my college graduation was 1978. As a graduating senior with a solid GPA and as co-chair of Wesleyan's black student organization (Ujamaa), I had been asked to give the invocation at the commencement ceremony. 1978 was also the year that the majority of black students at Wesleyan decided to stage a sit-in at the office of Wesleyan's president in protest against Wesleyan's investment in corporations that did business in South Africa—the fortress of apartheid at that time.

The dilemma I faced was whether I would express my anger over an ongoing system of racism through political agitation or suppress my anger by remaining neutral on the issue of Wesleyan's investment in corporations that perpetuated racism. By staying neutral, I would appease the university brass and graduate with the distinction of being deemed acceptable enough to reflect the accommodationist mentality of an educated student body in the delivery of my invocation.

I wish I could say that I was brave enough to counter my instincts for institutional acceptance in favor of the fight for social justice. I wish I could even say that I placated the university hierarchy long enough to use my place on that graduation stage to say something about the responsibility of every person who has knowledge of an injustice to act urgently and to agitate forthrightly against it.

Instead, I followed the personally uneasy but politically safe path of visiting (not joining) the students who were standing up for justice by sitting in, while I continued my trek toward institutional sanction and individual distinction.

Suppression of black rage is the first lesson of black success in America. It is a lesson that I and countless other black Americans have learned, perhaps all too well.

It is the "talk" that virtually every conscientious black parent gives to his/her son or daughter, particularly in light of the prevalence of racial profiling and the "war on drugs," which is largely waged in black communities.

It is the reason why Barack Obama was not considered "electable" until he publicly disavowed his identity with and passion for the black liberation theology of Jeremiah Wright. Despite all of the obvious and subtle racial attacks against his person and his presidency, most black Americans admire the President and the First Lady for their calmness and lack of ostensible outrage. But while we admire President Obama for controlling his anger over injustice, we pray that he never loses it.

It is the reason why most black Americans celebrate the American dream of Martin Luther King. Jr., but viscerally identify with the American nightmare of Malcolm X. Malcolm reminds us why we should still be angry. Martin reminds us why we should still have hope. Without the bitter truth of Malcolm's diatribe, we would have little to fuel the fight for Martin's dream.

Conservative responses to any contemporary allegations of racism are well-rehearsed. Instead of combating "supposed" racism, conservatives contend that black Americans should focus on reducing the number of black single-parent households, raise our own children, stop our own black on black crime and get ourselves properly educated.

As the pastor of a predominantly black church in a predominantly black community, I can attest that there is no shortage of sermons, programs and injunctions in the black community that call black people to take personal responsibility for their economic and social plight. In most black communities across the nation, there is a plethora of religious and civic programs that speak to everything from economic empowerment to sexual abstinence to parenting skills to the importance of education. In fact, the largest, most prominent churches in the black community are those that completely eschew liberation theology and focus exclusively on personal piety and personal responsibility.

But the issues that plague black Americans and other marginalized people are not just a matter of individual responsibility. Those issues are also rooted in systems of institutional oppression.

Complete suppression of black anger at the systems and institutions that perpetuate injustice may secure individual advancement and provide us with privileged places on the stages of institutional acceptance. But since my college years, I've found my most Christ-like experiences to be the ones in which I've been denied social and religious acceptance because of anger expressed in campaigns to disrupt systems of bigotry and discrimination. Sometimes rejection is the highest honor.

QUESTIONS FOR DISCUSSION

1. Many believe that the election of President Barack Obama signals that America has now entered a "post racial" era, in which racism is no longer a critical issue. Do you agree?

2. What did the national response to former Los Angeles Clippers basketball team owner Donald Sterling's racist remarks reveal about where we are as a people in regard to racism today?

3. Many African Americans believe that the diminishment of the Voting Rights Act, the dismantling of Affirmative Action programs and the systems that drive the mass incarceration of black men are all contributing to the re-segregation of America. What are your thoughts?

4. Why are candid conversations about racism in America so difficult to have?

When the Church Doesn't Understand Addiction

Emily C. Heath

A few months into my tenure at my first parish, one of my parishioners rushed into my office looking panicked. "There's a horrible rumor about you going around town!" she warned me. "People are saying you're an alcoholic!"

On any given Sunday, looking out from the pulpit, I see the faces of addiction. I see addicts caught in a cycle of short-term sobriety and relapse. Parents hopeful that their adult children will finally check themselves into rehab. Recovering alcoholics with decades of sobriety. Couples who have "one too many" on most nights but "can stop whenever they want." Spouses who are coping with a partner's addiction. And, far too often, friends who remember someone who in the end died from a very real disease.

My church is not atypical. No congregation is untouched by addiction. In fact, I'd go one further and say that just about no family is untouched by addiction. But far too often we limit our conversations about addiction in the church to complaining about how the AA or NA group that meets in the basement left the heat on again. Meanwhile, all around us in the pews, addiction is an all-too-often unspoken part of the church's story. But spoken or not, addiction is what I see when I look out from the pulpit.

What many of those in the pews who look back at the pulpit don't realize at first is that when they look at me, the pastor, they also see the face of addiction. When that church member came to me in a panic to tell me about the rumor going around town that I was an alcoholic, I told her that the rumor was true. I am. I am a recovering alcoholic. That has been true for years for me now, ever since one morning in graduate school when I decided that I had had enough, and that I didn't want to go any further down the same road I'd seen family and friends take. Since that day, many 24 hours ago, I have not had a drink. And by the time I arrived at my first parish, I had been sober for years.

I am fortunate. I was never arrested. No job was ever lost due to my addiction. My insurance could have covered any treatment I needed. And when I told my family and friends that I needed to stop, the universal response was, "How can I support you?"

And yet, even now I write those words, "recovering alcoholic," with fear and trembling. I still worry "what will people think?" I hear the well-meaning advice of other clergy to never talk about an addiction history publicly if you ever want to secure a position as a pastor. I see the concern in a few eyes about what it means to have an addict as a pastor. What will people say? In my case I've found that people do talk. (The rumor going around my town, for instance, had started innocently enough. Someone had seen me at a recovery event.) But I've also found that people talk in other ways. They talk about their stories. They talk about their family's stories. They talk about what alcohol and other drugs have destroyed. And, every so often, they talk about the beauty of recovery.

These conversations rarely take place, though, without someone being willing to start the conversation with honesty and vulnerability. And sometimes that is particularly frightening to churches who do not like to talk about the hard and messy things. (That's most of our churches, by the way.) But once that conversation is started, the results can be amazing.

Several years ago a prominent member of the community joined the church I served. People were proud to count him as a member of the church. And one day they asked, "Why had you never come to worship with us before?"

His response stunned many. "I've been coming to this church for twenty years on Saturday nights," he said, referencing the weekly AA meeting the church hosts. "It's only recently that I learned I might be welcome on Sunday mornings too."

What I learned that day is that the church that does not openly speak about addiction hasn't just failed to welcome those who struggle with it. It also fails to welcome the Gospel message. We teach that falling down defines us whether or not we get back up. And, inadvertently, we've taught a sanitized, powerless Gospel.

And somehow we have taught that Christians are people of perfection, and not people of redemption.

Recovery from addiction is all about finding new life. This is not an unfamiliar message for Christians. It's the business of the church. And yet sometimes we are so reluctant to proclaim it.

A friend who works with a recovery program tells me that he struggles to find even a few open beds for the dozens who come to him telling him they want to get clean.

And so, for those who cannot get the treatment they need, including detox, rehab, and continuing counseling and support, two options remain: death or jail. Too many are lost to the first. And, contrary to the "war on drugs" rhetoric of politicians, there is nothing in the second that will treat the disease of addiction.

Changing the public discussion of addiction and recovery is going to take a cultural shift. It's going to take those of us in recovery telling our stories. It's going to take demands for more funding for treatment centers. It's going to take communities working together to advocate for recovery-oriented drug courts instead of more jail cells. It's going to take all of us saying, "This isn't working anymore . . . and it's time to break the cycle."

This is hard work. And this is holy work. And this is church work.

But in order for us to do this life-giving work, we've first got to tell the truth. We have to tell the truth about the stories of addiction in our pews. We have to tell the truth about what we've failed to say in the past. We have to tell the truth about the ways we have contributed to the judgment of those with addictions.

And we have to tell the truth about recovery, and the new life that God can give to those who seek it. We have to tell the truth. Because the truth will set us free.

QUESTIONS FOR DISCUSSION

1. How has substance abuse impacted your life? Your family's? Your community's?

2. Do you see addiction in your community? How has your church responded to what you see?

3. What does it mean for the church to proclaim a Gospel of healing to people in recovery?

We Always Find a Reason to Fight the Next War

Martin B. Copenhaver

I can tell you the exact day I became convinced of the absurdity of war—December 1, 1969, the date of the first draft lottery. I was only 15 years old at the time, but my brother was older, so he was in the lottery. They ran it like a game show. For every birthday there was a capsule in a huge bin. Someone would reach into the bin and read the birthday. The lower the number, the greater the chance you would be drafted and sent to Vietnam. I held my breath as each birthday was read, hoping not to hear my brother's birthday—November 4.

The show was run on network television, complete with commercials. Early on in the process, someone reached into the bin and read, "November ..." but before he could read the date, they cut to an ad for Norelco electric razors. An animated Santa, sitting on the head of a Norelco razor, slid down the hill as if he were riding a sled, all accompanied by the cheery strains of "Jingle Bells." My brother leapt from his chair and started screaming at the screen: "I can't believe it! My life is on the line and you're selling razors!" A narrator came on: "Christmas is a time for closeness—and closeness is what Norelco razors are all about."

It turns out that my brother got a high lottery number. But it felt like a close shave.

Today I have a stack of bumper stickers in my office that say, "I'm already against the next war." When someone expresses sympathy—or even amusement—with that statement, I hand them one of the bumper stickers. I think it reflects the Gospel of Jesus Christ. We are called to resist, not just any current war, but any war, including the next war, whatever that may be.

After all, this Lord and Savior to whom we have pledged our loyalty refused to enter Jerusalem and seize power through force. Instead of taking a throne of earthly power through force, Jesus chose instead to be lifted up on a cross. He refused violent means to power to accomplish his purposes and instead demonstrated that God deals with evil through self-giving, non-resistant love. It made no sense as we normally calculate things. But in God's design it allowed for the ultimate victory of the resurrection.

And Jesus makes clear we are to follow him in self-giving, nonresistant love. He says in his sermon, "You have heard it was said, 'An eye for an eye and a tooth for a tooth.' But I say to you, Do not resist the evildoer. But if anyone strikes you on the cheek, turn the other also . . . . You have heard it said, 'You shall love your neighbor and hate your enemy.' But I say to you, Love your enemies and pray for those who persecute you, so that you may be children of [God] in heaven" (Matthew 5:38-39, 43-45).

Some have concluded that Jesus here is setting forth an impossible ideal. And, to be sure, through the centuries some Christians have sought ways to qualify those words. But those who lived in close proximity to Jesus did not doubt he simply meant what he said. They assumed that Jesus' own response to violence was an example for them to follow. That is why, for the first three centuries of our history as a Christian people, it was simply assumed that nonviolence is a central and inextricable element of faithful discipleship.

Thomas à Kempis said 500 years ago: "All people desire peace, but few desire the things that make for peace." While we all say we want peace, we are more attracted to war than we normally admit. At the very least, we do not want to accept the changes that will make for peace. We do not want to give up anything of our way of life. We do not want to release our death-grip on anything that we have come to think of as ours. We do not want to see the world or ourselves from another's point of view. We do not want to give up the conviction that we are right or just. We do not want to forgive past wrongs or receive the forgiveness of an enemy. We do not want to give up ancient hatreds. We do not want to forget. And all of that, it seems to me, is cause for confession.

I wonder: Can we even begin to imagine a world in which our response to violence is something other than violence? Can we even begin to consider what it might mean to seek change and resolve conflict without resorting to armed force?

I realize that even asking such questions leaves me open to the indictment that I am naïve. Just for asking such questions. So let me be clear: I am not saying such an approach to change and conflict would be easy or without great cost. But when such questions are not even raised, I think you have to conclude that G. K. Chesterton was right: "Christianity has not been tried and found wanting; it has been found difficult and left untried."

When we spend 1.7 trillion dollars a year in attempting to bring about change through nonviolent means—which is what the United States spends each year on the military—and when such attempts are found fruitless, then perhaps we could say that nonviolent approaches are naïve.

When we have a Department of Reconciliation in Washington that is as well-funded as the Department of Defense, and it proves powerless to bring about change, then perhaps the label naïve would be accurate.

When we have deployed hundreds of thousands of our citizens who are willing to do anything—including sacrifice their very lives—to resolve conflict in a nonviolent manner (in other words, in the way we deploy the military), and find such commitment inadequate to serve the cause of peace and justice, then perhaps we could say that such an approach is naïve.

When we train our brightest young people in academies of peace-making that are as highly valued as West Point and Annapolis, when we glorify the difficult, patient work of peacemaking more than we glorify war—and if after a period of years and decades, all of that is found wanting, ineffectual, then perhaps we might be able to say that it is naïve to think that change can come about by means other than violence.

But until then, I'm with Chesterton: "Christianity has not been tried and found wanting; it has been found difficult and left untried." And that's why I'm already against the next war.

QUESTIONS FOR DISCUSSION

1. Is there a specific time when you encountered the horrors—or perhaps the absurdity—of war?

2. Do you agree with the assertion that everyone hates war? Or, do we always find reason to fight the next war because in some way we are attracted to war?

3. Do you think G. K. Chesterton's observation ("Christianity has not been tried and found wanting; it has been found difficult and left untried.") is applicable to war?

Quinn G. Caldwell is the author of the newly released *All I Really Want: Readings for a Modern Christmas* (Abingdon). He lives on a small homestead in Upstate New York with his partner, their toddler, and an alarming number of animals. He is the Pastor of Plymouth Congregational Church in Syracuse, New York.

Martin B. Copenhaver is the President of Andover Newton Theological School, Newton Centre, Massachusetts. He is the author of six books, most recently *Jesus is the Question: The 307 Questions Jesus Asked and the 3 He Answered* (Abingdon). Martin also writes for a number of periodicals, including *The Christian Century*, where he serves as an Editor at Large. Martin's other claim to fame is that he once made a television commercial with Larry Bird.

Jason Coulter has been the Pastor of Ravenswood United Church of Christ in Chicago since 2006. He is a former union organizer with the Steelworkers Union and the Union of Needletrades, Industrial and Textile Employees (UNITE!). Rev. Coulter was once arrested with other union activists at a demonstration and the woman to whom he was handcuffed later became his wife.

Lillian Daniel is the author of the best-selling *When "Spiritual But Not Religious" is Not Enough: Seeing God in Surprising Places, Even the Church*. Senior Minister of the First Congregational Church of Glen Ellyn, Illinois, her speaking engagements have taken her from Queens College, Ontario to Kings College, London.

Emily C. Heath is the Senior Pastor of The Congregational Church in Exeter, New Hampshire. She is a member of the national United Church of Christ Board of Directors, a speaker and writer on Christian faith and social justice, and a frequent blogger on Huffington Post.

Matt Fitzgerald is the Senior Pastor of St. Pauls United Church of Christ in Chicago where he lives in the Lincoln Park neighborhood with his wife and their three young children. He is a frequent contributor to *The Christian Century* magazine. In his younger years he worked at nearly every job a restaurant has to offer, from washing dishes to tending bar.

Matthew Laney is the Senior Minister of Asylum Hill Congregational Church in Hartford, Connecticut. A native New Englander, he has served congregations in Vermont and Michigan and worked with people who are homeless in Atlanta. Matt is a husband, a father and an aspiring novelist for young readers.

Mary Luti is the Interim Senior Pastor of Wellesley Village Church (MA). A long time seminary educator and historian, she is the author of *Teresa of Avila's Way* (The Liturgical Press) and numerous articles on the practice of the Christian life. She is also the former pastor of First Church in Cambridge (MA), the only woman senior minister in over 375 years of continuing congregational life. She is a founding member of The Daughters of Abraham, a national network of interfaith women's book groups.

Anthony B. Robinson is the President of the Seattle-based leadership development institute, Congregational Leadership Northwest. He is the author of a dozen books on leadership, congregational development, and the spiritual life, including the best-seller, *Transforming Congregational Culture*. He has been a featured speaker at many events and conferences across North America, most in locations you've never heard of.

Kenneth L. Samuel is the Pastor of Victory for the World Church in Stone Mountain, Georgia, and the author of *Solomon's Success: Four Essential Keys to Leadership*. He is Co-Chair of the African American Leadership Council of People for the American Way, Washington, D.C. and the proud parent of one daughter, Kendalle Marye.

Donna Schaper is the author of 32 books, most recently *Grace at Table: Small Spiritual Solutions to Large Material Problems*, and Senior Minister at Judson Memorial Church in New York City. She grows a superb tomato and has three children, two grandchildren and a husband whom she has known and loved for 32 years. A board member of the New York Civil Liberties Union, Schaper is an enthusiastic activist.